Writing Christian Fiction

by Ben Patterson
Copyright 2014 Ben Patterson

ISBN: 978-1-502-76568-0

Summary

Interested in writing Christian fiction? Author Ben Patterson offers tips, strategies, and counsel for writers getting started in telling stories from a Christian worldview. Included you will find:

–how to use the life of Christ as a model for story structure

–the five main character types

–the main conflict types

–the main story types

–the rules of handling point of view

–how to show and not tell

–some basic tips on usage

–a glossary of fiction genres

Whether you are starting out or want a refresher on basic elements in the craft of fiction, you'll find this an accessible guide in WRITING CHRISTIAN FICTION.

Getting Started

The way to write a book is to actually *write* a book. A pen is useful; typing is also good. But never stop putting words on the page. *Probably the best advice you'll ever get*. Be kind to yourself. Fill pages as quickly as possible. Regard every new page as a triumph.

However, first things first—in every story you need to know where you're going. No one packs for the Himalayas when their destination is Hawaii. Each and every story has a theme, a reason for existing. What is the theme of *The Three Little Pigs*? Wasn't it, 'Be prepared?' And *Chicken Little*? Was it 'Presuming without factual evidence can be costly?'

My story, *Neil Before God*, has as its theme, 'God's grace leads us to salvation.' *Teri with the Lord* is a David and Goliath story. Its theme is 'Perseverance has its rewards when God is with you.' *Shrek*'s theme is, 'Like yourself and be who you are.'

A theme is the writer's reason for his story; it's the moral. If you can summarize it in a sentence or two, then it's clear to you. If you struggle to define the story's point, then you haven't quite gotten it. Knowing your story's theme is stage one.

Stage two: Once you've decided on a theme, then choose a genre. Is your story present day, the future, the past, or even another world? Is it sci-fi, fantasy, a mystery (detective novel), a romance, historical fiction …?

Next, who's your hero, and where's he or she going? What? You thought working through these issues was going to be easy? There's no free lunch. Writing is work: it's research: it's thinking. And it's a great big gamble. Although you're essentially on your own, other people can help you; thus the reason for this book.

Getting bogged down is a huge problem for many writers, *novice* and *seasoned* alike. An otherwise good story never sees the light of day because the writing gets trapped in a quagmire of *what if*s, and *where should I go*es. Despite an author's best efforts, his story drowns.

How long can you slog through a literary swamp before you tire, falter, and then ultimately fail? Unless you're a masochist, plodding along in a slurry of possibilities with no clearly defined end in sight, can wear on a soul, and wear you out.

Consider, if you will, shark infested surf. It's easy to get eaten if you're just paddling around looking for some place to go. But what are the sharks' chances of making a meal of you if you're up on the board, rapidly skimming over the waves toward shore? I'd say, next to nil, my friend.

At a writers' conference a few years back, I sat down to lunch with a couple of attendees, both novice writers. One mentioned she was having trouble ever finishing any story she started. Before I could answer to advise her, the other, a silver-haired gentleman, said he used the *Yadda yadda yadda* method or some such thing (it's kind of a blur right now). Then he began to expound on the many and varied merits of this writing method.

I stopped him short to ask one simple question: How many stories had *he* completed?

"None," he answered. "I've been working on the same story for the last ten years. But it's coming along quite nicely." The man was literally beaming.

Not to be rude, but I couldn't help but laugh inwardly. "Her question was, 'How do I *complete* a story I've started,'" I reminded him.

Ten years with nothing to show for it? Sorry. That doesn't work. My advice to you is the same as it was to both those people: *know where you're going to begin with.*

Sure, there are rules to writing well, and we'll discuss those rules in detail later. But if, like our gentleman friend, you aren't getting it done, a rethink is in order. Indeed, for him, a rethink was long overdue.

There are two very important rules to writing:

First - Begin your day with prayer. Everything you write comes from the abundance of your heart. If God is there, if He has touched you even a little, this will show in your work. So, as a rule, each and every time you sit down to write, dedicate your work to our Lord Jesus Christ from and through whom all things were and are created.

Second - Know where you're going. If you have your theme solidly in mind, then write toward that end. I believe this is as important as is rule #1.

At this point, *do not* concern yourself with grammar, or spelling issues (you'll catch those errors later.) However, do bear in mind the rules for Point-of-View. While you may be able to keep your characters sorted one from the other, your reader will not be able to without your help. Train yourself think in and write in POV.

To simplify my life, I write one chapter after the other as individual doc files. Other than in special circumstances, I make every effort to keep each chapter in one person's POV.

When labeling chapters, I write them as follows: (101)description, (102)description, etc. This keeps them in order and helps me readily find whichever chapter I want when changes need to be made.

So what exactly is this story you've written? It's the initial draft; the framework—*the infrastructure*—to a completed literary work. No architect erects a building without first constructing a framework to give that building shape and strength. Writers, like builders, lay a foundation before building anything on it.

By thinking in this way, from the onset you'll anticipate something novice writers seldom do. You'll expect to make changes. Stories, as a rule, are ten percent written, and ninety percent edited.

Some writers are married to their work from day one. They are so in love with what they've put on paper, they'll accept no help or criticism at all. Yes, well, good luck with that. Only bad writers think that their work is perfect the moment pen hits paper. That kind of thinking keeps many would-be writers from ever truly completing a story.

Occasionally, novice writers, caught up in what they have written, believe they've just given birth to something that is God's gift to the world, and like a jealous parent, they are quick to take a defensive posture. Any suggestion that might hint their baby isn't fully developed is turned away out of hand.

But not you. You know you're not a parent who has given birth to a spectacular musing. You are a writer—*a craftsman*—who is constructing a work. In your effort to give truth scope, you, with words, build a container in which to place what you have to say.

Imagine a cabinet builder unwilling to hand his raw product over to a finisher to apply stain and lacquer, or unwilling to allow the hardware man to put handles, hinges, or drawer slides on. If such a man exists, does he beam over unfinished work?

Sure, our writing is God-given, but it's filtered through us, and *we* are not perfect. See your book as a team effort. First you, the author, lay the framework, the raw story, if you will. Upon that, eight stages of editing follow:

First edit - by you. You've finished the first draft. Walk away from it for a week or two. Work on another project, a sequel perhaps, or another new story. When you return to edit, you'll have a more objective view of it. Flaws will stand out, and you'll find it easier to edit. It'll be easier to create a better product.

Second edit – professional. Hand your story off to a professional editor. Having never seen your book before, he or she will have an objective opinion of your work which is a great advantage to you. A good editor will quickly discover your writing voice and help you hone it. He or she will also see common writing mistakes and teach you to watch for them. A good editor will teach you more about story telling than anyone else. It would be best to meet your editor personally to discuss your project.

Your first rewrite. You'll get your work back with MSWord's "Track changes" turned on and the editor's suggested changes. *You* will pick and choose the suggestions you want to keep and which you'll want to toss out.

Second Profesional edit. Manuscript goes back to the editor. The second look over will deliver more insight and a few more changes.

Now it's back to you once again for the second rewrite. Your writing is getting better, the story is coming into clearer focus, and you begin to see the true advantage to employing a professional.

Back to the editor for a final proofreading. Whether he or she personally does this or hands it off to a professional proofreader, the object is to find the errant punctuation, syntax, and spelling issues overlooked in the editing process.

Then it's back to you for its final rewrite before it's sent to the publisher.

The publisher, working closely with you, will reformat the manuscript for print, create a proper cover, and then give you your first proof copy. Look it over well; that's your name on the cover. It's your brand that's at stake. Approve nothing that doesn't fit your idea of an attractive, compelling book.

One word of warning, as you write, save your editing to the end. More often than not, *Edit-as-you-go* will sink your story. Second-guessing yourself throughout your writing is like pressing a pillow over your story and firmly holding it down until it stops kicking. When you're connecting pen to purpose, don't worry about getting it right—*just get it written.*

Once your story is complete and down on paper, or in MSWord, or wherever, then and only then is it time to edit, not before. Right now, you're that surfer slicing down a wave at incredible speed. Move so fast the sharks that want you for lunch haven't a chance to get more than a whiff.

Of the two writers mentioned above, the gentleman with the formula was more interested in getting his writing perfect from the get-go, paddling around thinking he was making progress as one shark after the next took a huge bite out of his time and energy. She, on the other hand, recognized that she lacked something important that she couldn't quite define. And unlike the gentleman writer, she was humble enough to ask for help … which I gladly gave.

I saw her some months later at a writer's meeting. She walked right up to me, gave me a big hug, and beamed as she told me she had finished her first story.

Lesson learned? Don't just *plan* to write. Write. It is only by writing, not dreaming about it, that we develop our own style. Over time, you'll learn the rules to writing and apply them without thinking about it. But for now, just write your story as it needs to be told. Write it honestly and tell it as best you can, as quickly as you can. Nothing that happens to a writer—*however pleasing, however tragic*—is ever wasted. When you are popping out story after story, others will be stupefied by your prolific ability.

Story Model

Christ's life is the most used story model today. His story covers all the elements that comprise a good plotline. Try to use the following elements as a guide. But remember, Christ's life serves only as a guide. You will learn that this story framework is flexible enough to handle anything from *Shrek* to *Titanic*.

The below bullet points are arranged in order to help you organize your thoughts and ensure your story has all the necessary parts to keep the reader interested.

The six basic elements in this structure are:

Jesus' birth - introducing your hero to the reader.

Jesus at twelve – a hint to future events.

Jesus ministry begins - committing your main character to make a change.

Mid-point - Reaching the crucial mid-point.

The Cross - Climax.

The resurrection – aftermath and impartation.

Jesus birth: introducing your lead character. Jesus was born in a manger, in a cave, to a carpenter and his wife. This was the humble beginnings to the greatest story ever told. His was a Cinderella, rags-to-riches story. This is Rose Dewitt-Bukater Dawson Calvert in *Titanic*, or Shrek in *Shrek*, or Malcolm Reynolds in *Firefly*.

Riches to rags is the inverse of this, as in the stories of *Coming to America*, or *Robin Hood*. In these stories a wealthy man assumes the guise of a commoner.

Likewise, in the first few pages of your story, show your hero living in his or her natural environment. From *this*, change is birthed.

This is who your hero was yesterday. This is the life he has been living for some time now. Do not show any of his flaws at this point. Do not establish a finish line at this point, either. Your hero's desire here is simply to continue living in peace.

In the movie *Shrek*, we find Shrek living in a swamp, his natural environment. He seems relatively content. He even makes a game of frightening the locals who come after him with pitchfork and torch. Though he's an ogre, he was delivered to the audience in such a wonderful way, you can't help but take an immediate liking to him. Getting the reader to like your lead character as soon as possible is vital.

Jesus at twelve: the evidence of things to come. "I must be about my Father's business." This is where you tease the reader by hinting where the hero's future might take him. In *Shrek*, Lord Farquaad dumps all the fairytale creatures in the swamp, Shrek's swamp. Initially, he hates all these uninvited guests. Their intrusiveness disrupts his life—*Donkey especially*—but these creatures serve as the hint to where the story is heading. Shrek never gets rid of the fairytale creature, but he does grow accustomed to them. And that's important to the story.

In your story, if you choose to make this change-of-direction a voluntary choice your hero makes, paint it as an opportunity that he finds attractive. This changed course might appear to your main character as a step up from what he's used to in lifestyle and/or environment — better pay, home, climate, or some other incentive. He enters the new life, and your hero acclimates to his new environment during this period.

Don't make this section of your book too long, but make it clear and concise. Most readers will want to get to the action sooner than not.

Jesus begins His ministry – A baptism. A desert journey. Tested by the devil. Gathering His disciples. Like Jesus' story, this is usually represented as a change in location as well: a trip, an adventure, or a quest. This is the part of your story where your hero commits to the new direction. This is the real road your hero starts down to achieve his goal. And this establishes the plotline. Though he never wanted to leave the swamp, Shrek begins an adventure to a strange new land.

In this section of your story, your hero faces his first real obstacles but rises to each occasion to handily defeat every trial brought against him. Each test should get increasingly difficult. Shrek faces bandits and a dragon.

Here your hero also identifies his enemies and gathers allies. As an example; in order to have his old life back, Shrek strikes a deal with Lord Farquaad to fetch Fiona. In Shrek's case, he realizes Lord Farquaad and his minions are his enemies, and Donkey, the dragon, the fairytale creatures, and Fiona are his allies.

Midpoint of Jesus' ministry – up to this point Jesus' popularity grew. Halfway through His three-year ministry, Jesus' popularity starts to wane. He knows this is the beginning of His march toward His crucifixion. At about the halfway mark your story's hardships and difficulties grow and may even disillusion your hero. He may want to return home to go back to the way things were. This will add tension to your story. But if your hero does go back, he must find no satisfaction in having done so.

As an example, Shrek delivers Princess Fiona to Lord Farquaad, then goes back to the swamp. But the swamp, a shadow of his old life, just isn't the same as it once was. Something's wrong with his old life that was brought to light by Fiona and Donkey, but he had to mull it over to figure it out. Shrek had to realize that his future didn't lie with those things he'd left behind but instead with the woman he had been with. Of course there were those mysterious and terrible *unknowns* waiting for him up ahead as well. In his hurry to get back to Fiona, he is near panic. Will he be in time to stop her farce of a wedding? Will she—*could she possibly*—love him as much as he loves her? He doesn't know. He knows embarrassment, ridicule, and rejection are most likely awaiting him. But he must find out, even if his chances are thread-thin in discovering if Fiona feels toward him as he does her.

For your hero, "Returning home" doesn't have to be physical. It can be just a state of mind. The hero may regret having made the move and simply dream of the way things once were, much like the children of Israel did after entering the wilderness. From here to the climax, tension must mount to urgent levels. Up to the midpoint, the hero has something he longs for but has only paid lip service to. Now he must commit to his goal. If he quits, you have no story.

The Cross – Jesus faces the ultimate challenge. He is tried, ridiculed, scourged, and marched to his own crucifixion. He dies and is buried.

This is the climax of your story. Your hero meets his greatest challenge here. To everyone—*the hero, his allies, the reader*—this scene must seem like an insurmountable, impassable wall. The situation must look as if it is hopeless. Do your best to write this scene as if the outcome has already been decided, and that your hero appears to have failed.

Despite what he faces, your hero has to make one last valiant effort—*to push through, to get the girl, stop the bad guys, to escape the pending catastrophe, recover the Pantelon jewel-encrusted crown of Firth, or complete whatever ultimate task you've assigned him*—or die trying.

Ask yourself what is the one thing your hero absolutely will not do, then have him do it. Shrek was secretive about his loneliness. He hated rejection—depicted as pitchfork, hoe, torch, men on the hunt, and Farquaad's taunts—so what do the writers of *Shrek* do? In front of a crowd of citizens, they expose him to ridicule, laughter, and taunting. And yet, to win Fiona's love, he pushes through his fears and overcomes them.

A friend of mine said we as writers create decent, goodhearted people, then we deliberately drag them through broken glass. *If* you want yours to be a story worth reading, that is indeed what you will do to your hero and his companions.

Hollywood actually calls this part of the story the crucifixion. Funny. They get that close, but miss the mark, the reality of Christ.

The resurrection and impartation - Your hero returns from his quest changed, and this change is evident to everyone. In the end, the hero should have sacrificed something of himself—his self-concept, or to some degree, he has been physically diminished. In getting through this ordeal, he has undergone a kind of purification where the last illusion of the hero's idea of himself is finally burned away. He is reduced to his pure essence—who he actually is. This change encourages others around him. This is evidenced well in *Shrek*. The other fairytale creatures see his changed attitude and now consider him a friend.

The reader must be allowed to experience the emotion that comes with the success or failure. The hero can achieve his goal, change his mind, get half the goal, as in *Titanic*, or the hero gains his goal but dies, as in *Gladiator*. Or the hero can even lose his goal and dies (a Shakespearian tragedy). The goal must be clearly resolved, and the reader must be allowed to respond emotionally. Ideally, the reader, stunned, slowly lowers your book to think about all that has transpired. Hopefully, he or she has grown to love your hero.

Like Jesus' disciples, the hero, having realized who he truly is, begins his new life. His view of himself has changed from his "Identity" to his "Essence" so to speak. This story may be left open-ended. The main issue is resolved, as are most of the minor issues.

If you intend to write a sequel, leave one loose end. Make it small enough to allow the reader the satisfaction of knowing the story is done, but large enough to leave your reader believing there might be more to come.

The changes in your hero may change those around him as well. Just as Jesus imparted the Holy Spirit to His disciples, your hero should impart something of himself to his allies and friends.

In the beginning of your story, your hero may have been indifferent to the poor or indigent. At the end, he might care for them in ways only you can imagine.

One California College studied a large number of popular movies to discover what made them work so well with the audience. They also looked at those that didn't fare so well. I was impressed with how similar some of their findings were to key points of Jesus' life. To make your life as a writer easier, what I've given you is the honed down version of their findings.

When the high-budget, much anticipated, first-ever *Star Trek* movie came to the big screen, the only thing that carried it was expectations. But an incredibly high percentage of *Star Trek* fans—*me among them*—found ourselves *under*whelmed. In trying to create an intellectual masterpiece, Roddenberry fell short of true entertainment. *Star Trek, the Movie*, lacked true suspense and excitement and had a nemesis we could neither like nor loath.

Movies that employ all the above to make for excellent viewing entertainment are: *Shrek*, *Titanic*, *Cars*, *Limitless* … just to name a few. I recommend *Limitless* as a good study. It uses this framework perfectly. As you watch it, see if you can identify where each of the above stages begin and end.

Although flexible, the above story outline is thorough. Enjoy.

Story and Element Types

The following is a checklist to help you identify and clarify key elements of your story.

Note: All great stories are love stories, especially when we see God as Love.

In all stories, the hero has two journeys he must take; a physical journey, and a spiritual journey. The spiritual journey changes your hero from Identity (how he sees himself) to Essence (who he is when all false fronts are burned away).

Character Types — There are five basic character types:

Hero
Reflective person
Romance character
Nemesis
Catalyst - Note: not every story has this character type. Just know it exists.

The **Hero** is the story's main character, the one who follows the foremost plotline.

To ingratiate your hero to the reader, you should employ _two or more_ of the following:

Attractive – Your hero's *character* should be captivating, involving the reader emotionally. He ought to be someone we can empathize with. Make this character likeable: a kind, goodhearted person who is liked by other people in the story. And/or . . .

In jeopardy – your hero may be threatened with: loss of life, limb, business, or job; or with pain. And/or . . .

Humorous – Possibly make him funny, amusing, or comical. And/or . . .

Victimized – Make this character sympathetic, such as a victim of some undeserved misfortune. And/or . . .

Skilled – Make him very good at what he does, or even powerful. A skilled businessman perhaps, a super hero, or computer geek. And/or . . .

Goal oriented – He should pursue some compelling desire or goal that has a finish line that we can imagine. In pursuing that goal, there must be seemingly insurmountable obstacles. If it doesn't seem impossible for hero to get his goal, we don't care.

In the end, the hero has been changed from his "Identity" (who he thought he was) to his "Essence" (who he really is after all the superficial nonsense has been washed away).

The **Reflection person** – is the sidekick. This is the character who is most aligned with the hero. The reflection person's objective is to help the lead person achieve his goal. He is the character who reveals to the hero his inner conflict. The sidekick keeps the hero on track, sometimes saying, "This just isn't you. This isn't like you. You're not being yourself." In Shrek, this is Donkey. Like a mirror, the reflection person shows the hero who he or she really is. He also serves as the hero's sounding board, in order to stay on track.

Conflict can arise between the reflective person and the hero, and for a time the reflective person may become the hero's worst nemesis. Sometimes if that happens, reconciliation is not only impossible, but downright objectionable. Beware! It takes skill to craft that sort of conflict and keep it believable.

The **Romance character** – This is the object of the hero's sexual or romantic pursuit. This person sees the hero's *essence* and falls in love with that. Write your story such that your hero and romance character stand in conflict at the level of *identity* and connect at the level of *essence*. She or he is the reward for the hero's moving out of identity (his protective persona) and into essence (who he really is).

The **Nemesis** – Do not confuse *nemesis* with *villain*. Anyone who opposes your hero, good or bad, is the nemesis character. This person embodies the hero's inner conflict.

As an example; your hero faces a visibly more power enemy. His choice to stand and fight or run may depend on those around him willing to fight alongside him. Any member of the hero's own team who feels strongly enough to oppose the hero can rise up and become a nemesis character. When some lesser character's goal stands in opposition to the hero's goal, a nemesis is revealed and rises to make known the hero's inner conflict. These conflicts also create tension, expose to the reader the true situation at hand, and help differentiate friend from foe.

Can a nemesis be a villain? Absolutely. Just don't limit your writing by making that always the case.

Catalyst – a character whose sole purpose is to elicit change in others by his or her unrecoverable injury or death. A catalyst must be crucial to everything that takes place afterword. The reader must find him or herself emotionally attached to this person, and feel the pain, or loss, of this character.

Plotline Archetypes

The plotline is the series of actions that take your characters from the beginning of the story to the end. There is always one main plotline which is set by your Protagonist, the main character. Frodo, in *Lord of the Rings* is an example. He has to destroy the one ring or die trying. There are several subplots which the lesser characters follow. Each one wants something. They fall under four basic archetypes:

Win something.

Escape from a place or situation.

Stop something bad from happening.

Retrieve something valuable.

To **Win** something, your hero has to have a set goal in mind: a prize, a girl, or whatever. This can be a contest, such as a game, tournament, race, etc. There is always something at stake if he loses, and great gain if he wins. Sometimes the hero loses the goal but wins something far more valuable: self-esteem, the recognition of *his* hero, and the admiration of his peers. As a subplot, this would be limited to a lesser character. In *Lord of the*

Rings, Legolas and Gimli's rivalry stemmed from a desire to get the greater body count.

To **Escape** from something or situation means the hero may have been unjustly imprisoned. Maybe he is hunted by a murderer or a vicious animal or enemy soldiers. He could be trapped in a dead-end job, or in something weird like a computer matrix or tunnel labyrinth. As a subplot, this can be one minor character defecting to the other side to help or even to deceive your hero. It could be a woman joining a fight or an adventure to get away from an abusive husband, etc.

To **Stop** something bad from happening, this plotline might involve finding a soon-to-explode bomb, keeping an evil politician from gaining the presidency, or tying up an enemy fleet until help arrives. As a subplot, this might involve a baseball player bribed to throw a game, a linebacker who has found out that the next blow will kill the secretly sick quarterback, or a man who knows his friend is about to marry the wrong girl.

To **Retrieve** something of value could be a policeman trying to find an escaped prisoner, a special agent's effort to recover a stolen painting or ancient artifact, or a wrongly convicted man who is trying to clear himself and regain his good name. As a subplot, this could be a minor character's effort to recover some bit of technology he inadvertently left behind in the enemy camp. If it falls into the wrong hands … this could be depicted as a second but lesser plotline for the hero.

Main Conflict types:
    Man against man.
    Man against self.
    Man against nature.
    Man against God.
    Man against society.

Man against man (hero against nemesis) is the most common conflict archetype. Remember that the nemesis isn't there just to create conflict, he is your tool to reveal your hero's character to the reader.

Man against self is usually the subplot in a good story. It is the inner struggles your hero has to overcome: fear, arrogance, pride, lust, addiction, what-have-you. It is a story of self-discovery, finding out exactly what one is made of when push comes to shove.

Man against nature is usually depicted as being lost in a snowbound wilderness (Been there, done that.) While this may have made a good story in the past, such themes have been greatly exhausted. Use it as a subplot. You may want to force your hero and his band to take shelter in a bear's den (hopefully without waking the bears). To reveal your hero to the reader, an unexpected icy blizzard can achieve this quite nicely, creating all kinds of opportunities. If your hero has to overcome noonday heat and humidity while fending off an aggressor, this can add tension to an otherwise dull scene.

Man against God is a common theme which never gets old. It is what we all struggle with. This can be your main plotline as in *Neil Before God*, or a subplot as in *Teri With the Lord*, or *Doug in Deep*. Learning about God and coming to understand certain truths about life as a follower is what we as Christians live for. God as a subplot, depicting Him as someone actively moving in the background, can increase a story's relevance and *point* a thousand times over.

Man against society is usually depicted as an escape, or acts of terrorism, as a rebellion, or as a conflict of ideologies which change a nation. It can be a plot to take over a country from within. Or writing a story about something as simple as trying to fix a broken school system can reflect a nation's attitude as a whole. The simple concept of *Pay it Forward*, an idea started by a young boy, had an impact that spanned the nation. *Pay it forward* is now part of the American vernacular.

Story Types

There are three basic story types: not to be confused with plotlines. While the plot is what defines your hero's goal, his physical journey, his **story type**, defines your hero's inner journey.

Your hero might **stand up for who he truly is** regardless of what other people think. He or she might take the risk of being who they truly are despite pressure to fit in. The story line might take the form of the hero conforming but tiring of doing so. Over time he discovers who he truly is and makes his stand.

Your hero might **risk connecting with other people** by giving himself to others, as in *Shrek*. A loner, he tries to avoid rejection by isolating himself. He convinces himself that that is exactly what he wants. But to win Fiona, he has to risk exposing himself to public ridicule and rejection.

Your hero might **commit to do what is right**, to do the moral or honest thing, to stand up for the truth and say, "Regardless of the consequences, I've got to do this because it's the right thing to do." This is usually depicted as building up over time when he reaches a point where he can take no more. He has to do the right thing.

One word of warning; if you're a novice writer do not try to employ every concept in this book all at once; take baby steps. See what each does in turn.

Point of View

When I started this venture, I had no idea there were rules to writing. Point-of-view (POV) came as quite a shock. I saw confusion written on the faces of those trying to sort through my work—*everyone found following my stories difficult*. It was missing a critical element in good writing. Along with other writing rules, I learned about POV and just how important it is in making a story clear.

The human mind is amazingly fast. It drinks in the world around it, processes the perceived data with blinding speed, and filters out the unnecessary and trivial. If we find a book in which the words flow readily from the page and hold our interest, we'll recommend it to others. However, if while we read our mind repeatedly stumbles over confused writing, tripping here and there, we assess the value of the thing and determine then and there whether it's worth any further pursuit. If it's a poorly written book, we set it down and move on to something new … oh, well.

An easy-to-follow storyline free of stumbling blocks helps the reader get into your story and grasp the point you're trying to convey; your story's theme. All too often a novice will write for himself instead of for the reader. While bouncing from one character's thoughts to another's might be clear to you, the writer, it will only serve to confuse your reader.

Movies inspire some folks to write. However a movie is an erroneous model for a book. Both tell a story, but each has its own set of rules to convey its message. Novice writers often fall prey to writing a book using movie rules. However, the written word presents a story quite differently than a movie. In a movie, the story is told by whoever is in front of the camera. Unlike a movie, to avoid confusion a book's storyline is told by one character at a time. That character is the POV person.

On the surface it may appear that movies have every advantage over the written word, but surprisingly, books can do what movies cannot. With the written word, the author can voice the thoughts of a character— get into what motivates him or her. But if in a book's single scene the reader can hear every person's thoughts, the reader will succumb to sensory overload. He may find himself reading and re-reading a single scene to sort out which thought belongs to whom, and what is actually taking place. Too much of that, and your book will be set down, never to be picked up again. More importantly, it will never be talked about positively or recommended to others. Learn POV and folks very well may find their selves standing around the water cooler asking others, "Hey, have you read . . . ?"

One such book that took off like a rocket was *The Shack*, and all because of word of mouth. It was one of the few books my Pastor recommended from the pulpit.

The following is an example of a story whose writer has given no thought to POV. To help you, I offer the following; a story that doesn't follow any one character's point of view:

Leslie and Stella entered the café. "Alright! I'm all up for an omelet," she said, taking her friend's hand to pull her toward an open table. They slid in to face each other.

She rolled her eyes, and pursed her lips to keep her breakfast down, which had only been a cup of coffee an hour earlier. She felt her face drain. Her hand grew clammy.

"You okay?"

"Ugh, bacon. Let's get out of here."

"Stomach bothering you?"

Jumping to her feet, she hurried for the street.

Rats! Blasted bacon got me hungry. With a shrug, Leslie sighed and followed Stella out.

Her stomach had been bothering her all morning. Stepping into the sun to take a deep breath, the nausea quickly fell away.

From behind, Leslie spoke with half interest. "You okay?"

Her heart sank a little. She hated tearing her friend away from her favorite diner, but she was helpless to fight what the aroma had suddenly done to her. Now she didn't even want to feel Leslie's touch, and mindlessly pulled away.

Was she ...?

Later that day, Leslie sat next to her friend in the exam room. *We could have had the results a dozen times over by now.* "This test was supposed to be quick and simple. What's keeping him?"

Stella clutched her friend's hand to comfort her, and leaned to whisper. "Take it easy. It hasn't been *that* long."

"It's been an hour."

"He has other patients. Will you relax? This could be good news … couldn't it? You did want to spend time with the girls, didn't you?" *That was a stupid thing to say.* Her chair was uncomfortable and Leslie's had even less padding. *Come on, Doc. Where are you, anyway?*

Just then Dr. Reinhert stepped into the exam room, and keyed up the computer. "Okay, let's see what we have here. Right! As I recall, several months back I told you that it was virtually impossible for you to get pregnant, Stella. Remember that?"

"How could I forget?"

"Hard to believe I could have been *that* mistaken."

"Dr. Reinhert, you mean . . .?"

"Congratulations, Mom. Have you thought about how you'll tell your husband?"

Okay, reader, did you lose track of who was saying or thinking what? While the above might be clear and understandable to the writer, the reader can quickly lose his ability to follow.

So as writers, we use Point of View (POV) rules to make clear who is saying and doing what to make the story easier to follow. Or you can write "she said," or "she thought," after each sentence, but even that would quickly grow old.

Rule one: The first character mentioned in a chapter holds the POV camera. She can pass that camera (the POV perspective) to another character, but only under certain conditions. More on that later. In the example below, Leslie is mentioned first, so this scene is from Leslie's Point of View. Although this is initially reinforced by "she said," the verb isn't always needed. Try this:

Leslie and Stella entered the café.

"Alright! I'm all up for an omelet," Leslie said, reflexively taking her friends hand to tug her toward a nearby table.

Rule two: Only those things in the POV character's range of vision can be written about. In this case, Leslie cannot see behind herself unless she turns to look. If she can't see Stella, she can't know Stella has rolled her eyes.

From the corner of her eye, Leslie saw Stella's face grow pale.

"You okay?" Leslie asked as Stella's hand grew clammy.

"Ugh, bacon. Let's get out of here."

Rule three: She knows only what is in her own mind, not her friend's. Unless you've written her as such, the POV character is not a mind reader. Leslie cannot know Stella's stomach had been bothering her all morning unless Stella had said something.

Though they had been friends a year now, Leslie had never seen Stella react to any fragrance quite like this. "Stomach bothering you?" she asked, hoping whatever it was would soon pass.

Stella released her hand. "Let's just go, okay?" Turning, she headed back out into the street.

Rats! Leslie thought. *Blasted bacon got me hungry.* With a sigh and a reluctant shake of the head, she turned to follow her friend out.

Rule four: A change of scene can mean a change in POV. In this case, as they leave the café, the POV can switch to that of Stella to give the reader a chance to hear her thoughts. To warn the reader that a change has taken place <u>leave a sentence space *blank*</u>. This scene will begin in Leslie's POV then switch to Stella's.

Rats! Leslie thought. *Blasted bacon got me hungry.* With a sigh and a reluctant shake of the head, she turned to follow her out.

— (Leave this space open.) —

Stella stepped into the sun and took a deep breath. The nausea quickly fell away.

From behind, Leslie spoke with half interest. "You okay?"

Stella's heart sank a little. She hated tearing her friend away from her favorite diner, but she was helpless to fight what the aroma had suddenly done to her. Then another thought popped into Stella's head. Was she …?

Rule five: Another way to shift POV is to create a shared experience that lasts long enough to allow the reader to forget whose POV it originally was. Written correctly, you can swing from one person's point-of-view to the other's and back again, without breaking the flow of the story or making the reader aware you've done so. The object is to keep the reader on track, so steer clear of overusing this.

Later that day, Leslie sat next to Stella in the exam room. *We could have had the results a dozen times over by now*, Leslie thought. "This test was supposed to be quick and simple," she groused. "What could be keeping Reinhert?"

Leaning to whisper, Stella patted her friend's hand. "Take it easy. It hasn't been *that* long."

"It's been an hour," Leslie mumbled in irritation.

"He has other patients, Leslie. Will you relax? This could be good news … couldn't it? You did want to spend time with me, didn't you?" *That was a stupid thing to say*, she thought. She was uncomfortable in her chair, and knew Leslie's chair had even less padding than hers. *Come on, Doc. Where are you, anyway?*

Just then Dr. Reinhert stepped into the exam room, and keyed up the computer. "Okay, let's see what we have here." He tabbed twice more and studied the screen a moment before turning to her. "Right! As I recall, several months back I told you that it was virtually impossible for you to get pregnant, Stella. Remember that?"

"How could I forget?" Her heart sank a little further.

A faint but unmistakable smile curled the corners of Dr. Reinhert mouth. "Hard to believe I could have been *that* mistaken."

Stella's mouth dropped open. For a moment, she couldn't speak. "Dr. Reinhert, you mean …?"

31

"Congratulations, Mom," he added. "You are very much with child."

Written in this way, the story is clear, the reading effortless. And to think, it only took a few centuries for writers to figure out what worked in making the story flow from the page. POV is key and crucial to keeping the reader on track without his having to "figure out" what was being said by whom, or whoever was doing the thinking.

There are rules to good writing, and all of them are for the sake of the reader, your customer, your bread and butter, your new best friend.

Show, Don't Tell

Tell us a story, said Jake. Telling a story has its place, but to draw the reader in and get him or her involved, we need to **show** them the story instead.

You sit down with a friend one day for a little one on one. You want to find out more about them so you coax them to tell you what they did in the Army or whatever. And they do what any normal, red-blooded American would do; they tell you their story.

Soon, however, you find yourself growing bored, possibly drowsy, as they drone on and on about who knows what while you get lost in your own thoughts. *That* is telling a story.

Consider the following:

It was cold and dark, and Janus stood by a crackling fire he had just built. He was edgy and flinched at every nighttime sound. He was tall and burly, and his fur cloak made him look bigger than he actually was. His friend, Cagle, had gone off alone to do what men do alone in the woods, and a twig's snap announced his return. Janus jumped at the sound and pivoted, pulling loose his sword. But his arm got caught in his cape, which had been gathered by the wind, trapping his arm before his blade was free. He was now vulnerable to attack.

But instead of the beast they tracked, Cagle, his traveling companion, stepped from the shadows to move closer to the fire. "Were I the ogre we chase, Janus, I could have easily killed you."

Janus jerked his arm free of his cloak, growled at his friend, then turned back to the warmth of the fire now well ablaze, stretching out his hands to it. "Blast this cold wind," Janus said as he vigorously rubbed his palms together. Then he held them out once more to the flames.

Cagle agreed, "Aye. Bitter cold it is. That much is certain. Not even my tunic keeps the chill from me."

Suddenly Cagle stiffened and sniffed the air. Then he slowly drew his sword from its sheath.

Janus scowled. "What is it?"

"I'm afraid, Janus, that we are now the hunted."

Did the above look well written? Told this way, just the facts are given. There is no tension, or urgency in any of this. A real yawn, if you ask me. An entire book written like the above would give your reader reason enough to nod off.

Telling your reader a story will certainly show the reader what is happening, but they'll only be a disinterested observer. You want them engaged, fully drawn in, and experiencing the scene with your characters. As a storyteller, your objective isn't to take the hero on a journey, but instead to take the reader. It's always best to show your story rather than tell it.

In writing your story quickly, perhaps you've written the above, and that's fine. It's only a rough draft. Now it's time to go back and change what was told into something that's experiential. After clearly picturing in your mind's eye the world in which your hero lives, set the scene up by painting the cold wind as a character itself—something the characters have to act upon and react to.

Start the scene with the POV character, and paint what he sees, hears, smells, tastes, and feels. It is only through that person's senses that the world around him is understood. Narrating puts the story in the narrator's POV and since he's not actually in the scene, he's as uninvolved as your reader will be if he has to plow through this. (Refer back to the chapter on POV.) Be careful. Everything you mention must have some significance in pushing the story forward. If you say there's a gun on a mantel, then it had better be used in some way and at some point in the story.

Remember: the scene itself is a character, a character to which every person must either respond to or fight to ignore.

A twig snapped! Janus jumped to his feet, pivoted, and pulled at his sword—his cape, gathered by the wind, trapped his arm before his blade was free.

Cagle stepped from the shadows. "Were I the ogre we chase, Janus ..." he said wearily, and shook his head.

The barbarian grinned crookedly and jerked his arm free of the cloak. He could see the irritation in the new arrival's face but could offer nothing more than a meager growl as a reply. Janus turned back to the fire which flicked, popped, and spat at his outstretched hands. "Isn't it enough the gods give us this northern blow? Must they fill it with daggers as well?" Janus vigorously rubbed his palms together before holding them out once more to the flame's warmth.

Stepping up beside his friend to the campfire, Cagle agreed, "Aye. Even through this thick Tulvin hide the wind stabs at me bitter, but—" He suddenly stiffened, and simultaneously sniffed the air as he slowly drew his sword.

Janus caught the foul odor now overpowering the pine, and reflexively gulped. "Me thinks there be more than one."

"Aye. Stand ready, Janus my boy, *we* have become the hunted."

Notice that the words "cold" or "chilly" are not used to describe the wind. It is only by their reaction to it that we see and understand what they're up against. It isn't enough that the characters chat, and interact. Their surroundings have to impact them as well.

Striker yanked the joystick to one side. Fighting the pressure of the turn, he strained to look behind his jet, all the while his neck muscles complaining of the tight maneuver. He jerked the stick back and instantly felt his stomach drop between his toes and blood drain from his face. At the edge of blacking out, he snapped the stick over, leveled off, and ducked into a cloud. But did he lose the MIG?

And don't forget to employ your every sense, including your nose.

Darrell stepped into his place of business, a woodshop on the Upper East Side. His men, already hard at work, gave him little notice. Maplewood and mahogany hung in the air nearly masking ... *what?*

Darrell raised his head and sniffed. Something disturbing was on the air. Something out-of-place. Different. But faintly familiar. It niggled at his apprehension.

Bothered, Darrell inhaled again, and looked around. No one else seemed to notice the odor that had instantly set him on edge. He went to the spray room, and peeked in. Joel was applying the final coat of forest green lacquer to a window sash. Even through the paint fumes, the alarming smell was stronger here. Then Darrell noticed the oily rags tossed into one corner of the room. "Irresponsible fool!" Smoldering, the rags burst into flame.

Meadows, forests, factories all have distinct fragrances, temperatures, sources of light-and-shadow; so when writing about such places, remember to capture every sensation that affects your hero and the people with him. Walk into a woodshop. Note the smell, the dust, the noises of machinery or a radio playing in the background. Use these elements to set a mood. Have a character notice his surroundings to give your reader a better sense of who the man is and what he faces. A Ninja assassin might even hear the cockroach skittering along the baseboards in search of food.

But be realistic and true to your characters. Eliminate anything that isn't necessary which impede the flow and progress of the story.

One last thing: you, *the writer,* should be invisible to the reader. Your only real presence is that of a narrator, and even in that you must remain invisible. Suzanne Collins, *Hunger Games* author, does a great job employing Katniss as the story's narrator from beginning to end. I, on the other hand, change the POV character with every chapter (occasionally several times in a chapter), and the scene is narrated from the POV character's perspective, *whoever* it might be. Regardless, unless this is an autobiography, stay out of your book. Be invisible.

Options

Once your story is written (First draft), go back and find areas where you explained a character's motivation and highlight them in red. Once that is done, consider each one in turn. Contemplate the following excerpt from my WIP (Work in Progress.)

"I am sorry," Mr. Portman said with expressionless eyes as he studied Jake. "You're right, lad. I don't know you, but I do know God. And I know what it's like to live a hard life. I joined a bloodgang when I was fourteen. I sniped my share of Enforcers, and I watched close friends die beside me. Some of those kids were younger than me. We thought we were part of some great resistance movement," he hesitated, glancing at Billy before focusing more intently on Jake, "but I was only a hoodlum. All of us boys were only petty hoodlums who lacked direction. *That* is the life I lived until I realized there was a better."

Jake dropped his head into one hand to rub his brow. "I was in a bloodgang on Atheron." He looked up to meet Portman's eyes. "I watched friends die as well. Where was God in all that?"

"He was right there beside you, Jake. All you had to do was shift your eyes."

"I just don't know how, Mr. Portman. I've done pretty well relying on my own wits, and I'd be doing alright now had it not been for ..." Jake hesitated, then abruptly pushed himself to his feet. "Listen. Thank you for lunch, Mrs. Portman, but I must be going."

"Sit down," Billy said softly. Up until now, Jake's mentor had remained quiet. He looked up at the younger man. "We have no place to be. Come on, sit down."

Jake sighed. "I don't think—"

"Please, Jake. Sit down." Billy's tone was calm but firm.

Jake glanced at the others, then reluctantly dropped once more into his seat.

"I was an Enforcer, Jake," Billy said softly. "You know that. But what you don't know is why. Had it not been for my brother's death, I'd probably be a freighter captain or something. My brother, Matthew ... my older brother ... my *only* brother, was an Enforcer ... and he was killed on Atheron by a bloodgang sniper. I joined the service for one reason and one reason only. I wanted revenge. Those punks who had taken his life didn't know that he was a medic ... an unarmed medic. I don't know that it would have mattered even if they did. To my brother, men were men, so he treated wounded soldiers and Bloodgang punks all the same. In his eyes there was no difference between them or us ... absolutely no difference whatsoever.

I once asked him why he did what he did, and you know what he told me? (Jake shrugged.) Matt said *he* was the resistance."

"He was," Jake mocked with a blasé tone. "All by his little lonesome, *Matt* was the resistance. Wow."

"Don't make fun," Mr. Portman said angrily. "A man lost his life. Don't make light of it."

Feeling a twinge of guilt, Jake glanced at Mrs. Portman, Mr. Portman, then turned back to Billy. "Sorry. I can be an idiot sometimes, Bill. Please, continue."

"No. Never mind," Billy said, giving in to his ire.

"Look, Bill, I'm sorry. Please, make your point. I'll give you no more grief."

Billy glanced at the Portmans before turning back to Jake. "Fine. What Matt said was, 'The resistance had to begin somewhere. If not with him, then with whom? He said violence begets violence and he wasn't going to share in that part of it …

… Until he died, I had thought he was right. Now that I'm a believer, I *know* he was."

[A thought popped into Jake's head; a memory of his one and only hardcore experience as a gang member. He and his pal Rocko had staked out a rooftop to await approaching Enforcers. "You never forget your first," Rocko had said with a grin.

As Jake scanned the streets with binoculars, Rocko sighted through his scope. "There you go," Jake had said. "Straight down McHenry. I count six head." Some four blocks away, down in the streets, an Enforcer patrol went from building to building harassing random pedestrians, rattling locked doors, and helping themselves to apples from a disapproving but cowed fruit vendor. Passersby did their level best to ignore them.

Rocko pivoted the rifle on its tripod, found a target, then as easy as cutting a slice of cake, pulled the trigger. It was just a slight pop—*surprisingly quiet actually*—but at the sound of it, Jake nearly jumped out of his skin. A soldier collapsed where he stood, the back of his head completely evaporated. "Right between the eyes," boasted Rocko.

Then just as cool as that, Rocko grabbed Jake's collar and pulled him behind the rifle. "Time to lose your virginity, boy," he said with an amused grin. "Go ahead. Take your shot."

It was odd. Like a movie in slow-motion, Jake recalled every little detail. He sighted, found his target —*a medic whose nametag read* TAFT. When he pulled the trigger, the Enforcer just crumpling like a sack of potatoes atop the man Rocko had downed.

Rocko was right; Jake thought. *You never forget your first kill . . . ever.* And that was *not* a good thing. Jake couldn't get the images out of his head: the man's face; the spray of blood coating the Enforcers who stood behind him; nothing.]

In the above rough draft, everything I've placed inside the brackets lets the reader know Jake killed Billy's brother.

This is interesting information, but it isn't written in stone. You still have options galore. This backstory can be moved elsewhere, altered, or deleted entirely. If this were your story, where would its best placement be; moved closer to to story's front, left where it is, or pushed back to appear later in the story?

To leave it where it is would create immediate tension between Jake and Billy. It might be better to pull out this part and place it deeper in your story, further back, to finally give reason for Jake's abrupt attitude change toward Billy. As the Prologue, it might serve to give reason for Jake's behavior throughout the story.

Consider this; how would Jake's attitude and behavior change if he suddenly realized that it was he who was responsible for Matt's death? In light of that, would Jake also see that he was responsible for Billy's subsequent entry into law enforcement? What would Jake do? Think about how *you* would respond and behave when you first spot your despicable deed and see it for what it is. Would you try to keep it from getting out? Jake wouldn't want anyone to know, would he? Would you?

You can also reveal this info to the reader, but not to Billy. Jake could confess what he'd done to the Portman's after Billy had left the house. Working it out with the Portmans could further define Jake, as well as reveal who the Portmans really are in Christ. With the Portmans sworn to secrecy, this knowledge could create more tension between the Portmans and Billy, as well as with Jake.

What would happen if Jake realized what he'd done, and blurts it out loud before thinking? What would Billy's response be, not to mention the Portmans'?

Bear in mind this particular backstory can influence your tale in a dozen different ways, and you might want to try several scenarios before deciding which is best.

This is your opportunity to further explain each person's character for good or evil, or highlight a certain person who you need to define better.

Be careful, though. A change made early in your story can and usually does change the direction of the story altogether. But if your goal is to write the most interesting, emotionally intense story ever, look for these opportunities with anticipation and you'll be happy with the outcome.

A Few Basics

Wordiness-
Reduce wordiness by changing:
"stooped down" to "stooped"
"rose up" to "rose"
"penetrated through" to "penetrated"
"caught sight of" to "saw"
"in the event that" to "if"
"at the present time" to "now" etc.
Also change:
"towards" to "toward"
"besides" to "beside"

Like/As If

The word "like" should not be used preceding a clause with a subject and a verb. Examples:

It felt like a furry ball.

It felt as if a furry ball rolled around in his stomach.

On the other hand, when "like" is a prefix... Follow with a hyphen when used as a prefix meaning similar to, e.g. like-minded.

No hyphen is used in words that have meanings of their own, e.g. likelihood, likewise, likeness.

Rise/Raise

Use "rise (rose, risen)" when you mean to move upward. Such as in: I rise to shake his hand.

Use "raise (raised)" when an object is being moved upward. Such as in:

Joe raised his foot.

Joe rose early in the morning.

On to/Onto

He held <u>on to</u> her foot. Use "onto" when you mean "to a position on" He tossed the spider <u>onto</u> the table.

To Lie/To Lay

The verb form of "lay" takes an object, and "lie" does not. Example:

He laid the shovel on the ground.

He wanted to lie on the ground.

Each Other/One Another

"Each other" is used when you refer to two people. Example: Mindy and John bumped into each other.

"One another" is used when you refer to three or more people.

Further/Farther

"Farther" is used to refer to physical distance.

She runs farther than I do.

"Further" is an adverb meaning to a greater degree.

I want further training.

Whoever/Whomever

To figure out when to use "whoever" or "whomever", substitute the word "he." If it sounds better to use "him," than use whomever.

In the two examples below;

1. It was as if whoever had killed them....
2. It was as if whomever had killed them....

"It was as if <u>he</u>" sounds better than "It was as if him," so use whoever.

Also note that "who" is the subject, and "whom" is the object.

Example: Whoever through the ball wasn't concerned with whomever got hit by it.

Since/Because

"Since" should be used when time is involved.

I have been sad since you arrived.

Use "because" when implying a cause.

I have been sad because my house burned down.

Insectlike/Insect-like

Precede "like" with a hyphen when the letter "l" would be tripled: businesslike, bill-like, lifelike, shell-like.

Precede "like" with a hyphen when the word has three or more syllables, e.g. intestine-like. Mississippi-like.

Precede "like" with a hyphen when the word is a proper name, e.g. Clinton-like. Exception: use Christlike.

Precede "like" with a hyphen when the word is a compound word.

Ellipses

Ellipses can be used to indicate a pause in dialogue or a trailing off of dialogue. If a complete sentence is fading, use four dots, with no space between the final word and the four dots. (One of the dots serves as a period.) If a sentence fragment is trailing off, use three dots, leaving a space between the end of the final word and the first dot.

Commas and Adjectives

Separate two or more adjectives with commas if each adjective modifies the noun equally.

They are brave, studious students.

This was a beautiful Persian carpet.

(Here "beautiful" modifies the Persian carpet.)

Participial Phrases

Modifying phrases that start with verbs ending in "ing" or "ed" require a comma before the phrase.

He pushed the ball, using a can of peaches.

Split Infinitive-

Some publishers ask that you don't put an adverb between "to" and "verb."

Incorrect: "to carefully create."

Correct: "to create carefully." (However, I tend to disregard this rule whenever it sounds "wrong" to my ear.)

Subjunctive

The subjunctive form of the verb is used to express something contrary to fact. Use "were" in all of the following:

If I were king...

I wish you were here...

It was as if I were...

Usually, "as if" and "as though" suggest a subjunctive mood. The following sentence (which starts with "if") is not contrary to fact so it is not subjunctive: "Jack didn't know what color the dog was. If the dog was black, Joe could find it in the snow."

Genres
Not all inclusive

Gen·re (zhän're; Fr.), n., pl. –res 1. A class or category of artistic endeavor having a particular technique, content, form, or the like.

Romance — stories that principally focus on love and relationships, and may take as a subject a single love relationship, or an individual looking for love. Often Romance will take place as a subtheme within another genre such as in a Sci-fi or in a Western.

Women's fiction — any story aimed to entertain women outside the *Romance* genre, i.e.: the story of a midwife, a caregiver, a wife dealing with an abusive husband, or the like. A story which promotes nurturing. Or a story bringing to light the difficulties women face.

Mystery — A story about characters that investigate crime or various puzzles. Time is a non-issue. Mysteries can as easily take place in the past as they can present day, or even in the future.

Science fiction — also called speculative fiction, uses scientific possibilities as a basis for a story, and might focus on things like apocalypse scenarios, post-apocalyptic Earth, future worlds, or space travel. In using time travel, this genre may incorporate historical fiction. In essence, this genre may speculate about the human condition, or about technology theory, or both.

Fantasy — deals with various "unreal" or magical things, or things not possible in the real world, and may contain alternate worlds and/or mythical and made up creatures or peoples.

Western — life in 19th-century America's Wild West as it was being settled; usually post-Civil war, and is often a type of historical fiction.

Horror relies on elements like the supernatural, apocalyptic events, or in some cases, exceptionally graphic cases of murder or mutilation caused by humans or other sources.

Thrillers — often called spy thrillers, have themes in which spies are involved in investigating various events, often on a global scale. This genre easily and often incorporates other genres such as sci-fi, romance, historical fiction, etc.

Historical fiction — Authors working in this genre invent characters for a specific time period and may tell the story of that time period through purely fictional and/or fictionalized non-fictional people as examples. A variation of this is the period novel, written either during or after a certain time period and particularly emphasizing what it was like to live in that era.

Game or sport — any story with a competitive game or sport as its backdrop. A story of this type may pit two teams against each other, as in *Facing the Giants* or *Rollerball*; one man against another, as in *The Champ, Rocky*, and *Thunderdome*; or one person against life's challenges, as in the movies *Walk Don't Run*, or *Arena*. A fictitious sport was used as a basis for the post-apocalyptic sci-fi books series *Hunger Games*, which pitted several teams against each other.

While the above is not an exhaustive list of genres, they are the most often used themes. Each can be geared toward an audience of children, adolescents, young adults, or what have you. Each can have religion, faith, etc., at its core.

Mixed genre — to combine two or more themes. For example, to add color and depth to a western, a writer might incorporate some romance; into a mystery, he might employ some horror; a Historical fiction might be in actuality, period women's fiction; etc.

Try to combine two or more genres equally and see what you can come up with. Consider the following examples: the '70s sci-fi/horror movie *Alien*; the romance/fantasy *Shrek*; the '60s TV series historical fiction/thriller *Wild Wild West*; to name a few. Though difficult, it can be done.

No matter: your genre, or genre mix, of choice, (the story's theme), sets the parameters for your storyline, and you must confine yourself to it or risk confusing the reader. Suddenly jumping from sci-fi (space) to fantasy (a magical realm) may prove a bit much to ask the reader to swallow. Though in theory this can be done, I know of no attempt that has had much success.

Sometimes genre doesn't matter. Two of my books, *Teri With the Lord*, and *Neil Before God*, are science fiction only because their setting has space travel as a backdrop. But because both are character-driven stories instead of plot driven, they could have just as easily been framed in a pre-twentieth century setting aboard tall ships; or even brought to present day on power boats. In the above-mentioned novels, *Celestria*, a spaceship that has the power to turn invisible, could have been depicted as an off-white sloop disappearing into a fog bank. Her crew might be able to follow the darker ships pitted against her, although she in essence would remain entirely invisible to them.

As a writer, the pictures you paint should first intrigue you. There's nothing wrong with writing stories for yourself. Identifying your audience is one key to writing well. No one should consider himself or herself unique, so by writing for your own gender and age group, you're sure to find an audience who likes and wants your stuff.

An issue to consider is: you should become an expert regarding your setting. Suppose you want to write a seventeenth-century novel about a ship's captain. You'll need to know the types of ships in existence back then, and in what region of the world in which they were sailed; the rigging, sail configuration, the name of each deck, the name of each below-decks room; that era's psycho-social mores a crewman might employ in his interpersonal relationships; etc. You can't hedge any of this. Your reader will find your errors and more than likely toss your book across the room in disappointment if you fall short of his expectations. So, do the research and get it right.

Did you know that in competition, accomplished author Louis L'Amour was the third fastest draw in his day; a Colt .45 was his pistol of choice. He loved the Old West and was considered an expert in that genre. But Louis L'Amour didn't just write westerns. Some of his works were present-day, now considered *era-stories*. But the fact was, he either wrote from experience, or from doing proper research. Don't shy away from following his example. Be the master of your genre.

Bonus Stuff 1

Recognizable Phases

The following is a list of phrases and scenes to help you in your writing. I would have appreciated something similar when I first started writing, so I've include this bonus material to help you. Turning a phrase was hard for me in the beginning, but as time rolled on, and I started to see each scene as an emotion, my writing improved. Feel free to use these. Modify them as needed to fit your story. But to make your book *yours*, you should try to develop your own. Writing well will come in time. Good luck and God bless you in your efforts.

– Ben Patterson

Facial Expressions:
She glanced at his hand resting on her shoulder, then gave him a look that made clear his touch was not wanted. It was then that he suddenly and painfully discovered his doing so wasn't even wise.

***

With her lips curled faintly into a smile, her eyes wanting to do the same, she sweetly said, "Come now, Captain. Certainly you don't believe everything you hear? I thought a man your age would know better."

***

His eyes followed her form slowly to the floor then back up again before resting on her pursed, red lips, her jade-green eyes. "You'll do. Next!"

***

Unable to focus, he knew his eyes betrayed him. He didn't have to tell her he had crawled back into the bottle.

***

Raising his right brow in mock concern, he studied the young man standing on the opposite side of the desk. There was a long moment of silence before he said simply, "Don't you think your veracity comes into question when you say such things?"

***

Closing his eyes tight, he pinched the bridge of his nose. "Please. Let's just move on, shall we?"

***

There was a moment—*brief though it was*—where she looked as if she could have killed him.

***

The harlequin face froze as John drew his 45. "Look here, Mime. I walk down this street every day. I'd like to do so without ever having to see your *over-the-top*, ill-advised antics. Understand?"

***

He must have had people he loved—friends, family, a sweetheart maybe—but the contempt in his eyes showed no sign that that had ever been true.

***

Taking in the sullen faces around him, he realized nothing he had said went over well at all.

***

She bit her lip. "There was an accident," she said, hesitating. A sheen of sweat beaded on her forehead as she tried to work around the parents' greatest fears. But her efforts were in vain.

***

"I had no idea how much I meant to you," she said, which brought a laugh from him and questioning looks from the others.

***

He looked around at their conflicted faces. Out of options, no matter what they tried, someone was going to die.

***

She pressed her lips together at the memory of her inept attempt at flirting, and of his smile after she had tripped and fallen into his arms. Nothing planned, but perfect timing nonetheless.

***

Then she noticed his amused expression and felt her own face flush with heat. *Why now?* she thought. *Why always with him?*

***

Ironic, encouraging, and a little funny, but not at anyone's expense, pastor's face turned red as he fought to keep from laughing out loud.

***

She finally appeared at the trail's foot, her face flush from running.

***

Body Language:

He pushed on the kitchen door and was met with no resistance. A thick wall of smoke billowed out.

***

As she caressed his face, she realized the whole thing was too twisted for a seven-year-old to understand.

***

Expressionless, he pressed his cheek to the scope, then twisted the end to focus through it. When the crosshairs lined up on the President's left eye, the gunman took a breath and held it.

***

She smiled benignly, then let the door close in his face. "Creep!" she whispered, turning to lean back against the door, relieved he had left without argument.

***

He gripped the doorknob; then, without turning it, he looked back with a mischievous grin. "I'm thinking the boys can win this one without me."

Her smile said she agreed.

***

As his fingers slid off her shoulder down her arm, her heart began to pound in her throat. She hated the way he had complete control of her, but at the same time she didn't want his touch to stop.

***

Without looking his way, she flicked her wrist to brush off his advice. "The door is that way. Be a dear, and use it quietly. Will you?"

***

She sidestepped the rock and ducked into the cave, out from under the snowfall, but froze at the sight of two golden orbs reflecting back out at her. A deep, low growl made her heart stop, sending a flight of panic up her spine.

***

He grabbed her wrist, stopping her fingers a fraction of an inch from the rocket's launch button.

***

Crossing one leg over the other, she folded her arms as she leaned back against her desk. Her brows leveled. "I'm not going anywhere, Sergeant. Not with you. Not with your men. Clear?"

***

Pretending the stiletto heel of her shoe was loose, she lifted her leg to reach back and wiggle it, her tiny dress rising above the knee as she did so. Then with a pout she dropped her foot. Had he noticed? He had. "The dance floor looks too crowded anyway," she said. "Can we just go?"

***

First curling her fingers toward her, then turning her hand out, fingers straight up, she studied her nails without looking his way. "Did you say something?"

***

"Buzz off," she said, and tried to push him back. It would have been easier to move a brick wall.

***

In full command, she kept her back straight as she lowered to the couch's edge, simultaneously turning her legs to one side, and subtly crossing one foot over the other. All the while her chiseled face masked any emotion. "If you insist, sir. But be prepared when our CEO sees it my way."

***

He brought his fists to his hips and scowled at his wife, though he knew there'd be no deterring her. Her mind was made up.

***

As if only an observer, he felt himself rise from his chair automatically to console her.

***

His fingers encircled the pearl before gently plucking it from its oyster. Holding it to the sky, he rolled it between his thumb and forefinger. Suddenly, he turned and tossed it in her direction.

***

Smiling like he had just won the war, the captain leaned back, and drew one foot after the other up to the desk top, each with a resounding thud.

***

He painfully pushed himself into a sitting position to direct his words at her. "You must go on without me. Save yourself. Save our baby."

***

She leaned on the table, her fingers spread wide on the wood grain. Her faint smile invited him to come closer and tell her what she meant to him.

***

She sat cross-legged on the floor to wait, and wondered if her mother would actually stay the night this time.

***

Additional – Visually Unclear:

"Yeah. Wait! What?" he sputtered, realizing he had been volunteered once more. Sure, it was a good plan—*a great plan actually*—but why did it have to be him out in front each and every time?

***

With the string still tugging at his hand, he knelt to pass it off to his nephew.

With folded arms and sour expression, the boy refused the kite. "What do you think I am, six?"

***

"License to kill?" he whispered as he considered the gun in his hand before looking at the body at his feet. "License to die, more like it."

***

Rattled by the turn of the conversation, she let her anger thrust her into her greatest demand.

***

Given the wealth of the patrons, it came as no surprise that most of the pretty girls in this church seemed more plastic than real—*except one*. A brunette sitting alone in the corner stopped him cold. She stared at him. He stared at her. Both seemed enrapt by the gaze of the other. *Breathe!* he told himself. *For goodness sake, take a breath*. But his body refused to do anything beyond drink her in.

***

He wanted to glare at her but felt it would be a mistake to take his attention off the approaching gunmen.

***

At the news her son had finally fallen asleep; she began to relax a little.

***

Their hands found each other. She tensed, realizing the very thing she fought so hard against was the very thing she needed—*his attention*.

***

"Why give in to them!" he snapped.

***

Eyes unblinking. She stands over his body as he rubs his jaw. "I'm sorry," he says, only now realizing the mistake he'd made in calling her that.

***

While he knocked down breakfast, he only half heard any of what she'd droned on about. Another day perhaps, but right now he had neither the time nor the inclination to give her the attention she sought.

***

Her heart pounded against her breastbone as her assailant's footsteps echoed in the hallway. Bursting through locked doors, he went from room to room searching for her.

***

If not dazzling, the dress was sufficient to turn a few heads. Such that her figure was, even had she worn sackcloth, the envy on every woman's face would have still been evident.

***

She wanted to make a few quick signs to the man standing across the room. But here, at this party for the deaf, there was no way to secretly express to him what she wanted to say. If someone saw, they'd understand her invitation as well. Then rumors would spread.

***

He hesitated, as if to consider the reliability of his own decision, and mindlessly shrugged. If only he surrendered, it certainly would simplify things. They'd believe he was alone.

***

After his moment of confusion, he chuckled at her wry joke, then at his own retarded reaction to it.

***

Trouble was, she did see. That much was written in her expression. And when she slapped his face, he didn't stop the blow from connecting, although he easily could have.

***

The wave must have been enormous, with tremendous power behind it. An entire apartment building had been washed into the lake. He stood and stared, unable to fathom the utter destruction that had swept by his house, missing it by mere inches.

***

She wedged herself between the tight confines of Scott and his date on the couch. The strong odor of menthol and eucalyptus separated them further. *Really?* He thought to himself. *A chaperone? Oh, yeah, this is starting off great.*

***

His eyes blurred. His head swam. All went black.

***

She poked around in the fridge, about to settle on leftover meatloaf, when he took her arm and turned around. "I had this hidden for a special occasion," he said. "Share it with me?"

***

All she wanted to do was to lie down in the nearby meadow and go to sleep. It was a shame that the last thing she'd ever see was the worry in his eyes as he pressed the gauze to her throat. "Stay with me, girl," he said, his voice sounding a great distance off. "We're almost there."

***

Still, he hated them. But, of course, he hated almost everybody now. Himself more than anyone.

***

"Your advice always seems to fall short of … *adequate*, Mister. And it always comes without request. Why is that?"

***

"Snap!" He spun at the sound, looked frantically for its source. Gun in hand, he searched for a target in the dark.

***

Without a word, he passed it over. She slipped it into her pants pocket where it clicked against her cellphone. They exchanged a look, and she knew he'd pursue her no more.

***

"Thanks," she said, her tone dripping with sarcasm.

***

From the balcony, she looked down at the tourists and hotel staff, and wondered if any of them would ever see their homes again. Forty feet high and coming straight at them, the wall of water argued against.

***

As everyone watched him walk through the crowd, he tried to appear extra calm to make up for his frantic heart rate. The moment he appeared, his bride across the room started toward him.

***

What was he going to do for company, whisper to the walls? He shook himself and slammed a clinched fist against the locked door. But he knew no one heard. The plague had left no one to hear … and him no way of escape.

***

This persona worked well in keeping him alive. Though they didn't care to, everyone tolerated his ramblings, believing he was as crazy as he made himself look.

***

With barely-bridled anger, the captain pivoted his chair toward the radioman. "The admiral isn't here, Corporal. He's seen nothing we've seen and doesn't understand what we're up against. Torpedoman … load all six tubes!"

***

Her words hung in the air for a long moment, no one knowing how to respond to such an outlandish notion. Truth be told, she was right, and everyone knew it.

***

His voice, forceful but calm, was quite effective as a ship's captain. But here … it only served to tick off his guest and annoy the other partygoers.

***

Her eyes instinctively searched for her husband, and she saw he had already gotten to his feet, apparently unharmed. The rumbling subsided.

***

She strolled up. "Ah, here you are," she said. The recent events had little effect on her mood. Even now, she was a rock of encouragement, a buttress of good humor.

***

"So much for setting an example," he said as he leaned shoulder to the post. "You shouldn't let her get to you like that."

***

It was all she could do not to slap him. His grin lingered as if to provoke her further. "Some men are *born* idiots," she said, keeping her voice calm. "But I see you are a self-made man?"

***

Taking a step back, he took a few breaths as if to calm himself. Then, without warning, he lunged, reentering the argument with fists and madness.

***

Her smile only served to confuse him more. What she said was cryptic. What she did was something else entirely. When she leaned toward him, he didn't know whether to kiss her, or respond to what she had just said. Like an idiot, he chose to do neither.

***

Guns were pointed, half at the captain, half at the major. Someone was about to die, when the major spoke up. "Keep the codes, Captain, and we'll all die together. Is that what you want?"

***

As he rubbed his stiffening neck, he realized there'd be no getting around it now. Someone was going to win, and someone was going to lose. He drew and released a breath before turning to the helmsman. "Take us in, ensign."

***

Jeff drew closer to the model to admire the intricate detail. Nothing more than a touch snapped an antenna off, which caused a sudden jerk in panic, sending the whole insect off its stand crashing to the floor. With wide eyes, its owner's jaw dropped, but he said nothing as Jeff awkwardly handed him the only item he managed to hang on to, the single antenna. Dusting his hands off, Jeff walked away.

***

It could've been meant as a joke if her tone wasn't so cold. Everything about her was wrong.

***

She heard voices and ducked lower into the shadows. A half-dozen men, one with a ring of keys jingling in his hand, passed her by mere inches.

***

His knee throbbed, his hands bleeding from breaking his fall. Dizziness swept across him, three days without a proper meal taking its toll. The flutter in his chest felt thin and weak, like a bird's heart instead of his own.

Fragrances:

When the old woman opened the door to him, he was greeted with air so think with mildew and cat urine it caught in his throat. Finding it impossible to breathe, he pushed past her to open a window, ready to break one if it refused to open—*if he could find one, that is.* Piled floor-to-ceiling, stacks of old newspapers lined every wall.

***

The unexpected spritz from the sample-perfume lady burned his eyes and throat. He spun. Saw her sinister smile. And realized a moment too late that she wasn't as she appeared.

***

Oil? Diesel? He turned to find a short, stocky, grease-covered mechanic standing in line behind him, and his appetite suddenly left.

***

The chemical stench of the apothecary took a little getting used to as John waited for his order to be filled. Maybe he was just overly sensitive—*maybe*—but in his thinking, everyone else was just too deadened to the world around them. Just then, like a knife, sweet lilac cut through the chemical barrier. He glanced back to see Miss DuMon window-shopping outside. Strange … no one else seemed to sense she was there.

***

He shut his eyes and let the paper drop to his lap. "Hi, Clarice," he said, knowing she had just come into the room through the door behind him. "Did you enjoy your bath?"

***

But after a moment of standing there, a tickle started in the back of his throat, and his eyes began to burn. Even an arm's length away, the spices were fiery enough to notice.

***

The press of bodies … the scents of cumin, paprika, and rose water mixed with the bitter pall of tobacco … and the heat of the noonday sun twisted his stomach into a coiling snake.

***

The tang of chocolate-tinged coffee seemed to invite everyone into the café from the street. Could no one resist its allure? With a certainty, he could not.

***

Instead of Said:

Below are alternative ways to say, "he said". Ninety percent of your book's dialog will have "he said," and that's not a bad thing. Don't try replacing every "he said" with these, but peppering this kind of language throughout your story will add color and character to your writing.

***

"Yes." John sounded hoarse. He cleared his throat.

***

John gave a discreet cough. "About done there?"

***

"He was tortured," John added.

***

"I'll take two." His words were very matter-of-fact.

***

Her mouth dropped open in shock. "What?"

***

"Is that all right?" Dumfounded, Jane just stared at him, so he repeated himself. "Honey, is that all right?"

***

He drew close and spoke under his breath. "Forget it."

***

"It's nuclear." Her words just hang in the air for a long moment.

***

"Get to bed," she scolded finally.

***

"Down!" she ordered.

***

"That's her," she heard someone hiss.

***

He read the letter aloud. "Dear John, …"

***

He saw a hint of a smile on her lips. "Not now, sweetie. After the kids are in bed."

***

"Will she ever quit," he whispered.

***

"When did he …" Her voice failed her.

***

John smiled. "You're going to be the best-dressed girl at the party."

***

John turned to his assistant. "Betty, you got all that?"

***

Her grandmother moved in on her quickly, framing her face with her hands. "My, what a sweet child."

***

"So well intended," John whispered in her ear, "but so insulting."

***

"Let's go," she mouthed. He responded with a quick shake of the head.

***

"Pick seventeen." But of what, she was vague.

***

The guard was abrupt. "You have the wrong floor."
***

Behind the door came a sound. Just a tiny whimper. "Please? Someone help me."
***

"Really?" John checked his notes. "I've got Two-Two-Oh-Three written right here."
***

"Who did this?" he pressed. "Was this your doing?"

"Did you request *this?* " she snarled.
***

"I honestly don't know." There's something in his voice that made Cindy believe him.
***

John turned to the guard who's just appeared at the cell door. "Why this? Weren't they punished enough, confined in this filth?"
***

Her brows came together as if she still tried to make sense of it. "No one would tell me a thing."
***

"Jan?" Bill touched her and she flinched. "Easy. It's going to be all right."
***

"It was a raid." John paused a moment, as if puzzled by her density. "You were to get out of harm's way."
***

John shook his head. "Don't push your luck."
***

John sat and put an arm around her shoulder. "Trust me. She'll be fine."

***

"You'll stay here," John told her for her own good.

***

John lifted the top page, revealing his schedule. "I've got testing at the pistol range next."

***

"They don't see … I mean, they don't know …" She got knotted up in her words.

***

She penciled in Ann's name. "Smyth, right?"

To consider this, John hesitated. "No, you're right. We'll leave first thing in the morning."

***

John nodded at Ann's plate. "I wouldn't let that get cold."

***

Ann countered his demand with one of her own. "Fine. But you'll sleep on the couch."

***

Ann took a stance, but this just made him laugh. "You can't be serious."

***

Delight ignited her eyes. "Look! Aren't these beautiful?"

***

John's face took on that distant look it wore when he was working something out. "Twenty-Three, no, Twenty-Four total, but there's no guarantee that'll get the job done."

***

"Right, you are. Check this out." John pressed a pad, the door hissed open. We followed him into the next room.

***

John smiled grimly. "If you knew everything Ann's been through this last year, you'd know how remarkable it is that she's kept it together this long."

***

John's hands closed around the perfect orb. "Natural? Not manmade? Unbelievable."

***

"Grip it lightly," John explained with a grin.

***

"Good bye!" Ann blurted out before slamming the door in his face.

Bonus Stuff 2

Hiring professionals:

My experience with saving money had cost me dearly. A friend once told me that we were too poor to buy cheap. Never a truer statement. Instead of new tires, I bought what I thought were good "Used" tires—a matching set of four that looked nearly new. It wasn't a week later when my right front right blew. The tread peeled away and beat the daylights out of the wheel well, right side of the car, and the front bumper. The result: the plastic trim ripped from the right front door; the front bumper—*also plastic and damaged beyond repair*—needed to be completely replaced; and the right front fender damaged with black rubber and paint removal. The cost of saving a hundred dollars? Over a thousand.

My first book: poorly written (as a novice writer, how was I to know) cost me more than two thousand in the end, simply because I didn't know who to hire.

I've heard similar tales from other victims, I mean writers, and so found it important to spread the good word; there is help. The following charge a fair fee and are well worth the savings you'll enjoy in the end.

Optimism Press
optimismpress@gmail.com
Book cover design, and content formatting.
Graphic art services, and publishing

Guide 4 Writers
Guide4writers@gmail.com

See L. Claire Smith for editing and proofreading services. Claire is a solid Christian who I trust without reservation. If you want quality work, you'll employ her services exclusively when it comes to editing fiction and non-fiction. Poets trust her, too.

Woodsong Studio
Lisa J. Swartzentruber, CPP, F.Ph.
Contemporary photography,
Digital Art and Digital Paintings
woodsongstudio@verizon.net
www.woodsongphotography.com

Lisa Swartzentruber, a certified professional photographer, is an Artist and does portrait work of almost any type including head-shots for Authors and book-cover work. She is a licensed business person living in Delaware.

Swartzentruber is an advanced Photoshop Artist and retoucher, and can create just about anything from a photographic file.

Graphic Artist
Taylor Patterson
taylorp@conssol.net
http:www.taylor-patterson.com

Contact Taylor Patterson for artwork, especially pencil drawing, and computer generated graphics. His pencil and mixed media art has won him the Delaware State Fair's *Governor's Award*, as well as the *Judge's Award*, and a full art scholarship at University of Delaware as a Visual Arts major. His work has graced several book covers, and he has illustrated book content for Guide-4-Writers and has contributed to book covers for Optimism Press.

Recently, Patterson's abilities won him a full scholarship to Venice, Italy, where he studied Oil Painting and Art History. Never a more deserving guy.

You'll love what Patterson delivers.

FAQ

As a writer, you might encounter the following questions during the course of your career. Preparing answers ahead of time will prevent you from becoming tongue-tied when hit with one of these verbal arrows. If you feel left out, don't worry. Once you get published, these people will jump out of the woodwork.

1. At Thanksgiving dinner, your cousin comes up to you, leans forward and speaks in a conspiratorial tone. "I have this great idea for a story. Would you be interested in working with me on it?" Before he launches into a lengthy and convoluted plotline, give this response: "I have more ideas than I can write, thank you, but I know another author who acts as a ghostwriter. He charges $10,000 per book. Shall I put him in touch with you?"

2. "I have a friend who's written a book, and she needs someone to edit it. She's desperate for help. Can I give her your phone number?" Let this person know that your services, if available, are not free. You would require a fee, a contract, and a waiver of liability. Or suggest she gain feedback by joining a critique group or entering a writing contest with score sheets. Another alternative is for her to hire a professional freelance

editor, but you still have to make clear it's a long road ahead. See Question Number 8.

3. You are in the doctor's office, and he asks your line of work. "Really?" the doctor says after you reply that you're a writer. "What do you write?"

"I write mystery novels."

"Are they, you know, published?"

"Yes, I've written over twenty books. You can buy them online."

"That's impressive. I've been thinking about writing a book. How do you get published?"

"You join a professional writing organization, attend meetings and workshops, go to writing conferences, and learn the business aspects of the career along with the craft. I'd love to talk more about it. How about if we exchange an hour of my time for an hour of yours?"

4. "How are your books doing?" is another question you might get from friends and family. Here's your answer: "They're doing great, thank you. Have you bought a copy yet?"

Another writer once told me she'd like to say her books had failed, she had entered bankruptcy proceedings, and did anyone want to help her out with some cash?

5. "Where do you get your ideas?" is a common question at book talks. Well, I pull them out of thin air, don't you? You'd think this one would be a no-brainer, but it's a question that genuinely baffles people. Ideas

are all around. It's having time to write these stories that's difficult.

6. "Are you making money at it?" I'd really like to reply, "No, I'm starving, and I need a loan." Many people think published authors are rich and famous. "I guess you earn a good living, right?" is another variation. Some folks will come right out and say, "So how much do you get for each book?" That's like asking your doctor, "So how much do you make on each patient?" I have a standard response: "I write because I love to tell stories. My advice to new writers: Don't quit your day job."

7. "I want to write a book, but I don't have time to learn the ropes. Can I pay you to write it for me?" See answer to Number One. Add a bit on the publishing biz and how writers are expected to spend time promoting their novel. Even if someone else writes the book for them and it sells, are they willing to put the time into marketing?

8. "Can you recommend a book doctor?" My answer: "If you're serious about becoming a writer, you'll learn how to edit your own work. All careers require practice and training, and writing books is no different. The only magic bullet is persistence. But you can hire a freelance editor to help you in the right direction. This still won't guarantee a sale. Plus, publishers expect more books than one work. You'll need to start on book number two right away, and be prepared to do your own marketing."

9. "Can I find your book in the library?" Librarians order books, so we want patrons to request them. But this question could be a good opportunity to launch into an explanation about the sources of distribution and the different formats for books today. You could counter with, "Do you like to read your books in print or on ebook?" And even if the person gets your book at the library, encourage him to write an online customer review.

10. "Where can I find an agent?" Hello, anyone hear of the Guide to Literary Agents? The AAR site online? Attending professional conferences? Entering writing contests? Let this person know about local writers organizations, classes, and seminars. They need to do their homework. And no, I am not going to introduce them to my agent.

11. "Is your book on the bestseller list?" This one is easy to answer: "Not yet, but if you buy a copy and tell all your friends about it, that will help me get there."

12. "Have you been on any talk shows?" The line is blurred here between the concept of an Author and a Celebrity. Becoming a published author may take years of learning, rejections, submissions, and rewrites. Celebrity equates to stardom. Serious writers work at the craft because they love to write. They know it is not an easy road to follow, and they're willing to put in the effort, suffer the indignities, and keep going regardless of whether fame or fortune come their way. Your answer: Repeat the one from Number 11.

13. "I've never heard of you. Are your books in the bookstore?" Again, this is a good opportunity to mention the various platforms for distribution.

14. "Any chance of getting your book made into a movie?" Realistic answer: "Unfortunately, it's not up to the author. The publisher may [or may not, depending on your circumstances] own the film rights. An agent might be approached by a studio or interested party who pays a fee to option the book. But even then, that might go nowhere. So the chances are slim for most authors."

Many of your answers will be individual based on your preferences. Consider every encounter an opportunity to educate the public about the publishing industry and what they, as readers, can do to help authors.

What we write comes from the heart. It's our personal expression, not ideas we pluck from someone else's consciousness or can teach in a quick lesson. Each person's journey is his own. We get where we are through hard work, grit, a thick skin, and persistence. Yes, I can offer tips and point wannabe writers in the right direction, but you have to be prepared to do the work. And you have to love telling stories.

So how would you answer some of these questions above?

Advanced Directives   Man vs (God)
                            society

Hero → to find who or what is killing his
                Patients
        skilled, likeable, goal oriented

To be confident in himself / (feel unsure
as a physician who has chosen the right
team   (stand up so
                        what is right)

Reflects- ~~xxxxxxxx~~   nurse LPN
                          keeps him

Nemesis- ~~xxxxxxxxxxxxxxxx~~
         ~~xxxxxxxxxxxxxx~~
    villian - Partner who
        believes in Deceying syphs
            Elderly population
    Celebrt - loss of a client interest
            to him
    Stop ~~xxxx~~ seal (loss of his ~~penalties~~)
        from lawyering   + nurse patient

subplot   ~~xxxxxxxxxxxxxxxxxxxxx~~
    2 nephew wins popularity
                Bible see?

        (mystery)

The Journey   skilled
clonless→   Good overall
Hero → to get to the City of Eternal

   ↓

                         Cards ordinary
To trust God + not his skill (as clk

reflective — Jim Fidel / Dan Hore

Nemesis - Boss   man
                                         vs
   Rovech - Jackford (Jason) lats)   society

      Escape carnal   (comt to
      ~~~~~~~~~~~   do
   end ship - ~~~~~~~~~   what's
              ess y re propan   right

      subplot
        ?

Cause Now in operation   Man
skilled, goal oriented, interesting   us   If started
                                     God   to work
                                            less/+
                                            now
                                            serious

Hero ———→ Find what really happened
              to his meats → + obtain a
                  Place in academy
    ↓
         Percus
To Find real meaning purpose in life in chaos

Reflector   Hotty-early Friend

Nemis — wife who
      Maks reality of God deep
         reality

~~team~~
Catalyst

Win something — researcher scientists
                + a tenured ticket

Subplot
      Side kick wing for a cluster / kinky
      Girl friend (? from ethiopia)

Caricature

Hero:
- to Find his ~~mother~~ Mother
- to "Be himself" only
- To Find a way ~~into~~ rose his life
- to overcome fear of as ~~cardinal~~ Goliath
- To gain confidence / be somebody less sophisticated
- To be someone who can commit ~~himself~~
- ~~in need~~ self sacrifice save christine / useless

Reflective - ~~uncle~~ Father / ~~princess~~ /

Nemesis — Lareue's son
  & Lillian

Romantic → Ela ~~letes~~ ~~on~~ more

~~deliight & his mother~~

- Retrieve ~~Accidentally with his Mother~~
    his Mom

① Rule
   comedy
   clones

② comit to
   do right

③ stick to
   wise
   Kelly
④

Stoplit ~~Timothy~~ Timothy:
  ~~Fast~~ Escape ~~that any~~ his
    "tell reputation
    by ~~Fingerbox~~

Fantasy

Milly children

Hero ⟶ to be popular

↓ lean -
integrity is better ren modernity

reflective ? Many Davy

Romance (little · old day in)

Nemeis - Demonic Qwral
    ↳ Joey - opposition slows
        in recceped of popularity at
        any cost

catalyst -

    win respect of freds
            & flegrl trivtins

    subplot   Recorge feels he
                stop (cannot - his)
                newry for Kees
                Mille for his destiny

in kleashe
Nunns
in Kerredy
7 thel micabd
mcn vs delf
(As what > right
or
woble
really
1)

CPSIA information can be obtained
at www.ICGtesting.com
Printed in the USA
FSOW02n1247050515
6936FS